Enjoy the Moment

Emilia Schreitmueller + Monique Fuchs

MAKING OF THE BOOK

Time is passing by so quickly and sometimes your head can spin with daily activities. So, we did an experiment trying to slow down, take a breath, and savor the little things that make us feel good every day ... and enjoy ... the moment.

We made the drawings and collages of our favorite moments and it took another two long years to complete this book.

But now ... enjoy the moment!

Emilia + Monique
Boston, November 2018

PS: The girl's name is Anna and the dog in the pictures is "Fluffi", our imaginary dog.

BUILDING A SNOWCAT

Building a snowcat is a lot like building a snowman. Just with whiskers, a tail, and ears. It is much fun. Probably other animals or things would also be good to build with snow.

READING STORIES IN BED

Stories are fun. Listen to them or have someone read them to you before you go to sleep. Maybe you will dream about them. And maybe you will mix the stories together in your dreams.

WATCHING FLOWERS GROW

Who said that watching flowers grow is boring? It is not. Try it at home - you'll see. Tulips do grow a lot in a vase.

SMELLING AND DRINKING HOT CHOCOLATE

Hot chocolate is so good. It looks delicious, smells amazing, and tastes very sweet. Whipped cream is kind of essential too.

CLIMBING A HILL AND WATCHING A SUNSET

Climbing a hill is a challenge. Watching a sunset is the best part. The clouds are pink and the rest of the sky is red, orange, and a little bit of yellow, and a little bit of pink.

SLEDDING ALL DAY

Snow is so cold. You can see your breath in the air. Going down the hill on a sled is fun especially with a friend.

DOING YOGA

Yoga helps to calm down. It makes you quiet and sleepy. It also can stretch your muscles and feel good.

GIVING HUGE HUGS

Give hugs to your family or friends or stuffies you love. You can also get hugs. Most are special.

PLAYING SOCCER

Playing a sport is fun. Although it would be more fun, if a dog or any pet can play.

FEELING THE GRASS

Feeling the grass barefoot is ticklish. It feels funny. It also smells good. The color is nice too.

WATCHING BIRDS

Birds are busy. They are fun to watch and hear. Sit still at a window and stare out. Maybe one bird stops and looks at you.

SINGING IN THE CAR

The car is one place you can sing loud. Nobody can hear you. It does not matter, if it sounds good.

MAKING CARDS

It is nice to make cards. People love getting cards. They will know, you thought of them.

EXPLORING NEW PLACES

It is fun to be in new places because you haven't seen them before. You can make new memories.

PLAYING WITH BALLOONS

They come in many colors and can make you smile. If you hang on to them they may make you fly. Letting the air out makes funny noises.

NEVER UNDER-ESTIMATE YOUR SUPERPOWERS

What are your superpowers? There are some moments when you can feel your superpowers. Celebrate and remember them and believe in yourself!

www.enjoythemomentbook.com

Illustration/Design: Emilia Schreitmueller/Monique Fuchs
Text: Emilia Schreitmueller
Artwork Photography: Tory Lam

ISBN: 978-1-7335624-0-9

©2018 by Monique Fuchs and Emilia Schreitmueller.
All rights reserved.

www.ingramcontent.com/pod-product-compliance
Lightning Source LLC
Chambersburg PA
CBHW040729150426
42811CB00063B/1543